Alphabet

Aa

A A A A   a a a

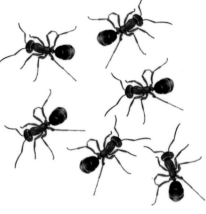

apple   hat   ants

Bb

B B B B   b b b b

Circle each letter **b**.

b d b
d p b
b d b

baby   ball

Cc

c c c c c c

crayons

car

Dd

D D D d d d

duck

digger

Ee

E E E   e e e

egg

elephant

Ff

F F F   f f f

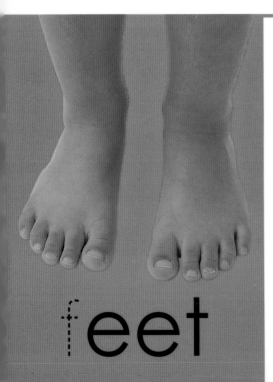

feet

flower

fish

Gg

G G G   g g g

goat

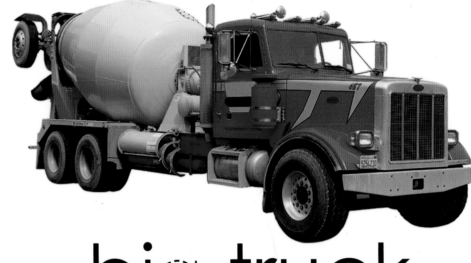

big truck

Hh

H H H   h h h

ouse

horses

Ii

I I I I   i i i i i

tw i ns

i ce
cream

i ll

Jj

J J J J   j j j j

j acket

j ump

j uice

Kk

k k k   k k k

Circle each letter **k**.

k a o

n k c

o k n

kitten   kite

Ll

L L L   l l l

snail   lion

Mm

M M M M   m m m

Cross out each letter that is not an **m**.

m w m

n m w

m m w

muffin   moon

Nn

N N N N   n n n

onion   nails   swan

Oo

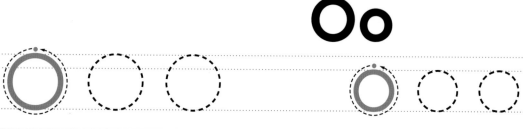

O o o   o o ig

owl

orange

spoon

Pp

P P P   p p p

paints

pig

Qq

Q Q Q   q q q

Draw a line
between each pair
of matching words.

queen
    quilt
quiet
    queen
quilt
    quiet

queen

quiet

Rr

R R R   r r r

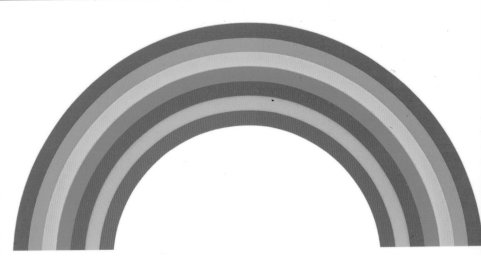

rose

rainbow

Ss

S s s   S s s

sandwich

starfish

Tt

T t t   t t t

train

tiger

Uu

U u u u u u u

c u p

Circle each word that begins with the letter **u**.

under   bird

crab   up

ugly   egg

u mbrella

Vv

V v v v v v v

v et

v egetables

v iolin

Ww

W W W   w w w

Circle each letter **w**.

w v w

v m v

w w v

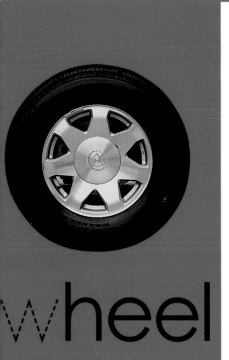

wheel

saw

Xx

X X X   x x x

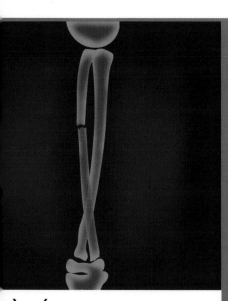

X-ray

fox

Yy

Y Y Y Y   y y y

yo-yo   yawn   yacht

Zz

z z z   z z z

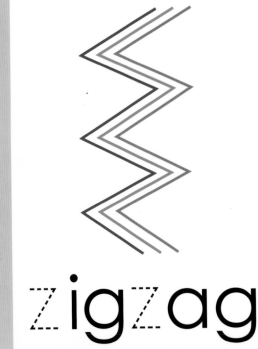
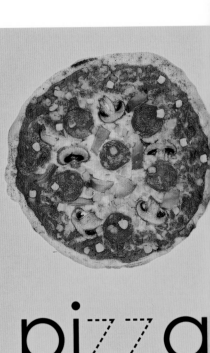

zebra   zigzag   pizza

Animals

Cat

Trace over the outline to draw the picture of the furry cat.

Food trails

Trace over the lines to feed the hungry animals.

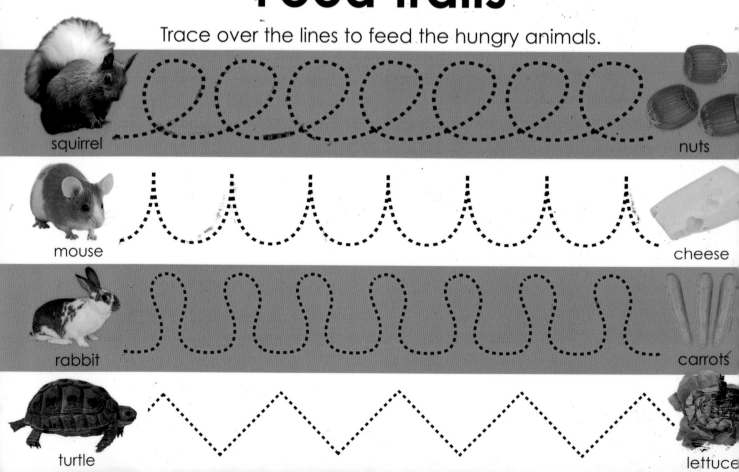

squirrel

nuts

mouse

cheese

rabbit

carrots

turtle

lettuce

Dog

Trace over the outline to draw the picture of the friendly dog.

Counting pets

Count the dogs in each area and write the numbers in the boxes.

Duckling

Trace over the outline to draw the picture of the fluffy duckling.

Farm friends

Use your pen to complete the farm animal activities.

Circle the two-legged animal.

Circle the two identical chicks.

Circle all of the lambs.

Cow

Trace over the outline to draw the picture of the big brown cow.

Matching up

Draw a line between each animal and the thing that it makes.

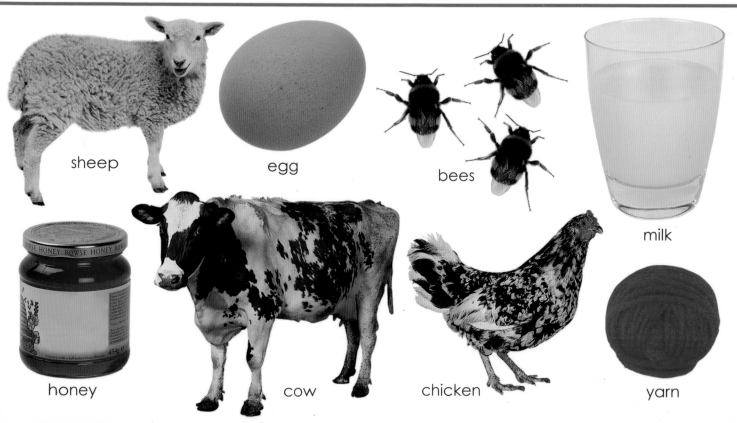

sheep

egg

bees

milk

honey

cow

chicken

yarn

Parrot

Trace over the outline to draw the picture of the noisy parrot.

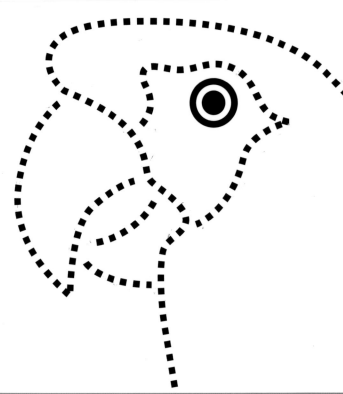

Animal colors

Use your pen to complete these animal color activities.

Circle the chicks that are not a normal color.

Circle the green animals.

Write the number of black animals in this box.

Fish

Trace over the outline to draw the picture of the swimming fish.

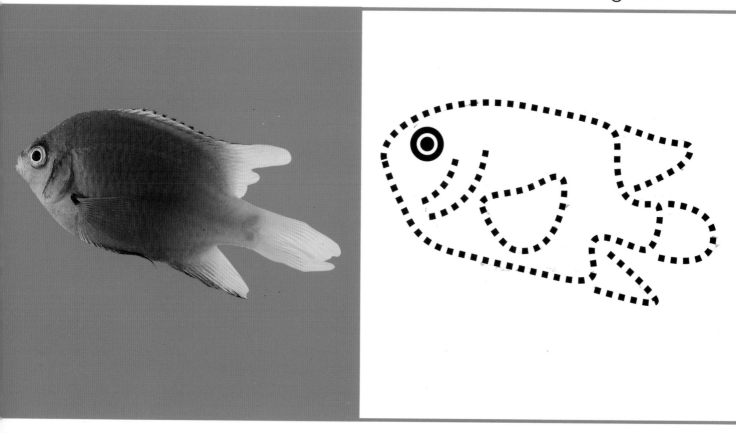

Missing halves

Can you finish drawing these animal pictures?

panda

owl

kitten

puppy

Butterfly

Trace over the outline to draw the picture of the beautiful butterfly.

Bee maze

Find a way through the maze from the bees to the flower.

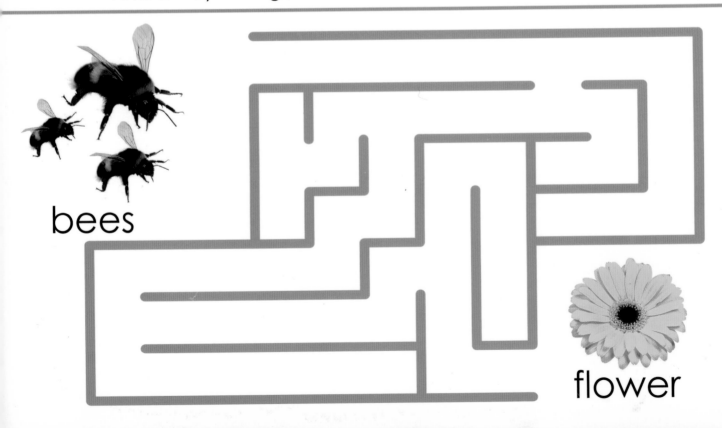

bees

flower

Animal sorting

Put an X on all the animals that don't have four legs.
The first one has been done as an example.

Fish maze

Draw a line through the fish from start to finish.

Time

O'clock

When the long hand points to the 12, it is something o'clock.

3 o'clock

10 o'clock

On this clock, the long hand is pointing to the 12, and the short hand is pointing to the 7.

The time is 7 o'clock.

Say the times shown on the clocks on the right.

Write in the o'clock times shown on the clocks below.

...... o'clock

.... o'clock

...... o'clock

What time is it?

Draw the long and short hands on the clocks
to show the o'clock times.

11 o'clock

2 o'clock

6 o'clock

7 o'clock

3 o'clock

8 o'clock

5 o'clock

10 o'clock

12 o'clock

One hour later

Draw the hands or write the numbers to show
the order of o'clock times in a day.

 ...... o'clock

 1 o'clock

 ...... o'clock

 3 o'clock

 4 o'clock

 ...... o'clock

 6 o'clock

 ...... o'clock

 ...... o'clock

 9 o'clock

 .... o'clock

 11 o'clock

What time do you . . . ?

Draw the hands on the clocks to show the time
of the day that you do these things.

What time do you get up?

What time do you eat breakfast?

What time do you go to school?

What time do you eat lunch?

What time do you eat dinner?

What time do you go to bed?

Five-minute steps

Each number on a clock stands for 5 minutes.
The long hand shows the number of minutes after the hour.

On this clock, the long hand is pointing to the 2.
The short hand is just past the 4.

The time is 4:10 (four ten).

Say the times shown on the clocks on the right.

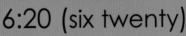

6:20 (six twenty)

8:35 (eight thirty-five

Write in the numbers to show the times shown on the clocks below.

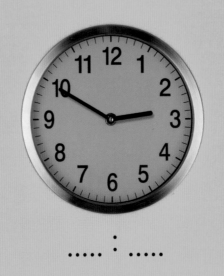

..... : .....

..... : .....

..... : .....

What time is it?

Draw the long and short hands on the clocks
to show the minutes after the hour.

3:35

8:10

1:45

9:15

6:05

3:10

10:20

6:30

5:05

30 minutes past

When the long hand points to the 6, it is half past or 30 minutes past the hour.

10:30 (ten thirty)

On this clock, the long hand is pointing to the 6. The short hand is halfway between the 1 and 2.

The time is 1:30 (one thirty).

Say the times shown on the clocks on the right.

5:30 (five thirty)

Write in the :30 times shown on the clocks below.

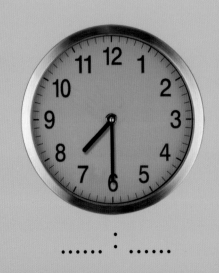

...... : .... : .... : ......

What time is it?

Draw the long and short hands on the clocks to tell the :30 times.

12:30

1:30

2:30

6:30

9:30

3:30

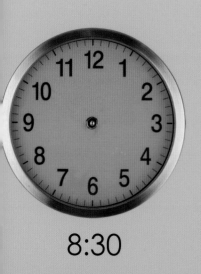

8:30

4:30

7:30

15 minutes past

When the long hand points to the 3, it is quarter past or 15 minutes past the hour.

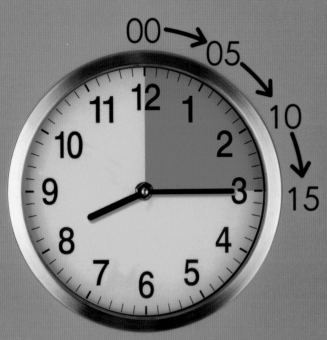

10:15 (ten fifteen)

On this clock, the long hand is pointing to the 3. The short hand is just past the 8.

The time is 8:15 (eight fifteen).

Say the times shown on the clocks on the right.

4:15 (four fifteen)

Write in the :15 times shown on the clocks below.

...... : .... : .... : ......

What time is it?

Draw the long and short hands on the clocks to tell the :15 times.

1:15

3:15

2:15

11:15

8:15

7:15

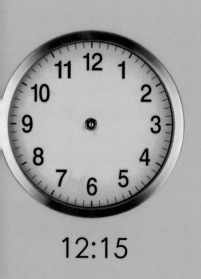

12:15

10:15

6:15

45 minutes past

When the long hand points to 9, it is quarter to or 45 minutes past the hour.

5:45 (five forty-five)

On this clock, the long hand is pointing to the 9.
The short hand is just before the 10.

The time is 9:45 (nine forty-five).

Say the times shown on the clocks on the right.

1:45 (one forty-five)

Write in the :45 times shown on the clocks below.

...... : .... : .... : ......

What time is it?

Draw the long and short hands on the clocks to tell the :45 times.

12:45

11:45

6:45

8:45

10:45

4:45

7:45

5:45

9:45

Digital time

Clocks that use only numbers to tell the time are called digital clocks.

12:00

11:00   1:00

10:00   2:00

9:00   3:00

8:00   4:00

7:00   5:00

6:00

6:00

6 o'clock

2:00

2 o'clock

This clock is showing 4 o'clock.

On a digital clock, it is shown as 4:00 .

Say the times shown on the clocks on the right.

Draw the hands on the clocks to match the digital times shown below.

11:00

11 o'clock

3:00

3 o'clock

10:00

10 o'clock

Numbers

1 1 1 1

1

forage
harvester

1
hen

1 barn

1 pig

one one

Can you match the baby to its mother?

foal   sheep   calf

cow   lamb   horse

2 2 2

2 lemons

2 strawberries

2 bananas

2 apples

two two

How many cherries are there? ☐

How many melon slices are there? ☐

Circle the things with two legs.

Circle the two fruits that are the same.

3 3 3

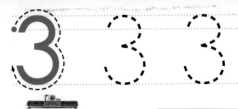

 3 emergency vehicles

 3 trucks

 3 tractors

 3 diggers

three three

| Circle each number 3. | Circle the groups of three dots. | Circle the shapes with three sides. |

4 4 4

4 party dresses

4 kids at a party

4 presents

4 balloons

four four

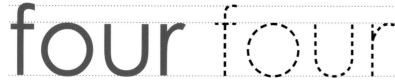

How many ice pops?

How many cupcakes?

Circle the four blue candies.

Circle the things with four legs.

5 5 5

5 red sailboats

5 swimming fish

five five

Connect the stars with five points.

Circle the five yellow chicks.

Circle each number 5.

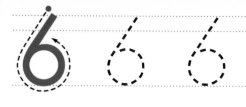

6 6 6

6 frogs

6 butterflies

6 dragonflies

6 snakes

six six

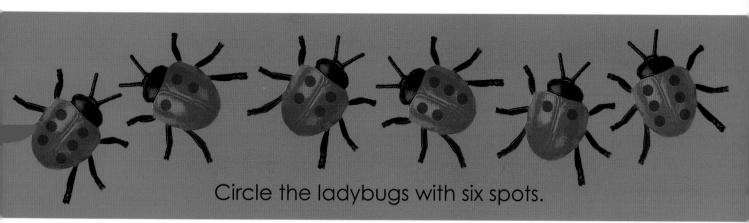

Circle the ladybugs with six spots.

Circle the bugs with six legs.

7 7 7

7 girls

7 boys

seven seven

How many yellow buttons?

How many hats?

Circle each number 7.

Connect each number 7.

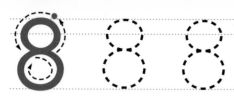

8   8   8

8 puppies

8 kittens

eight eight

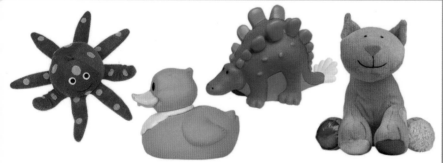

Circle the toy with eight arms.

Circle the eight green things.

How many birds are there?

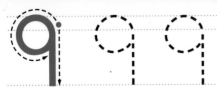

9 triangles

9 coins

9 decorations

9 gift bows

nine nine

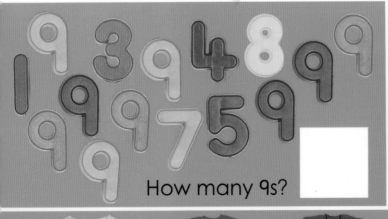

How many 9s?

How many flowers?

Circle the T-shirts with the number 9.

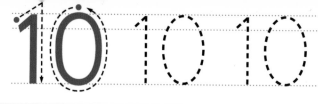
10 10 10

10 candies

10 donuts

10 chocolate eggs

ten ten

How many ice creams?

How many brown animals?

Circle the number 10 car.

11 to 15

Count the objects, and then trace the numbers.

11 inner tubes

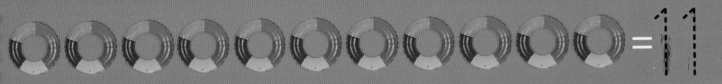 = 11

12 penguins

 = 12

13 leaves

 = 13

14 acorns

 = 14

15 flamingos

 = 15

16 to 20

Can you spot the odd item in each group?

16 socks

 =16

17 paw prints

 =17

18 flowers

 =18

19 pencils

 =19

20 peas

 =20

Count and draw

How many things are there in each group?
Circle the correct number.

3 5 1 8 2

6 9 4 3 7

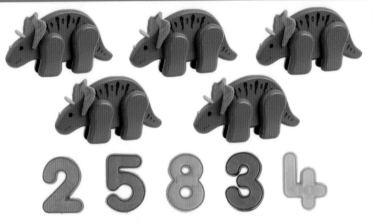

2 5 8 3 4

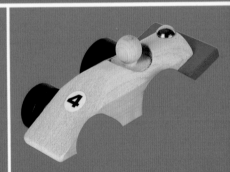

1 3 5 7 9

Draw five spots
on this dice.

Add one more
flower.

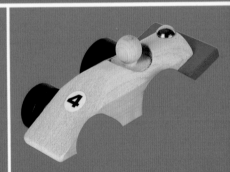

Give this race car
two more wheels.

Draw three candles
on the cake.

Give the teddy bear
two eyes.

Draw four windows
on the house.

Matching numbers

How many food items are there in each group?
Circle the correct number.

3 5 1 8 2

6 9 4 3 7

2 5 8 3 4

1 3 5 7 9

Number practice

Practice writing numbers by tracing over the outlines.

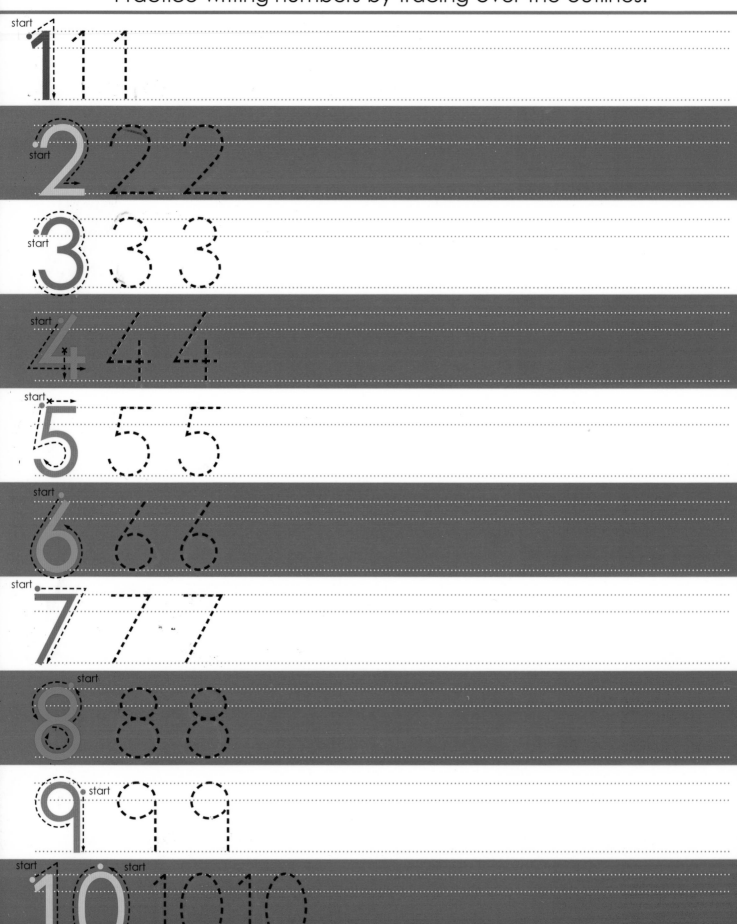

Spelling

abc

Letter practice

Trace over the outlines to practice
writing the letters of the alphabet.

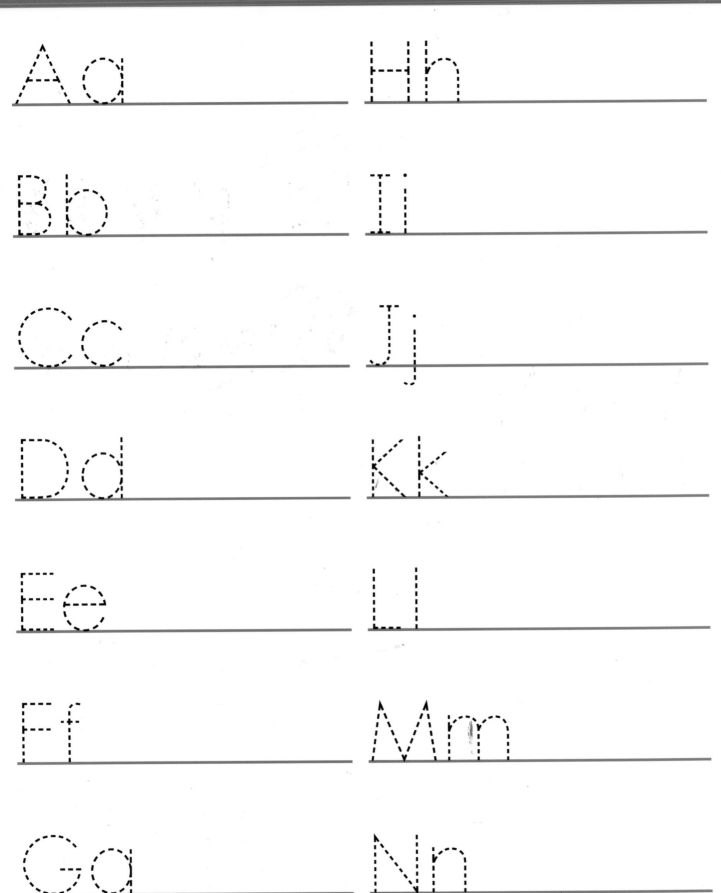

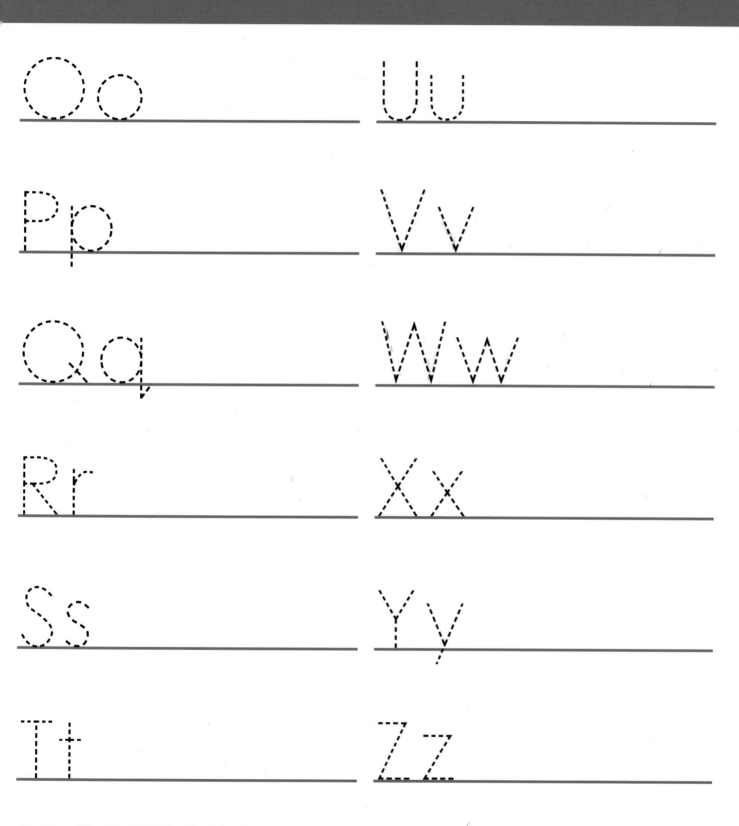

Oo   Uu

Pp   Vv

Qq   Ww

Rr   Xx

Ss   Yy

Tt   Zz

ABCDEFGHIJKLMNOPQRSTUVWXYZ
abcdefghijklmnopqrstuvwxyz

First letters

Write in the letters that make the first sounds of these words.

d og   __ird   __at   __ig

__ar   __ug   __abbit   __orse

__og   __un   __ox   __pple

First sounds

Circle the things that begin with the following letters.

Circle the things that begin with **t**.

Circle the things that begin with **d**.

Circle the things that begin with **m**.

Last letters

Write in the letters that make the last sounds of these words.

boa t

bir __

fro __

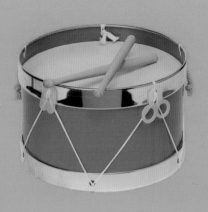

dru __

cra __

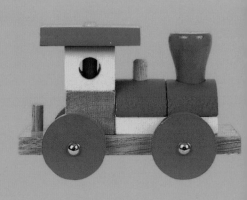

trai __

mil __

do __

cu __

Last sounds

Draw lines between the objects and the
letters that make their last sounds.

n Which things end with **n**? Which things end with **t**? **t**

p Which things end with **p**? Which things end with **s**? **s**

l Which things end with **l**? Which things end with **d**? **d**

Middle sounds

Use the letters **a**, **e**, **i**, **o**, and **u** to complete the words.

a

s <u>a</u> d   h __ t   b __ t   c __ t

e

p __ n   h __ n   t __ n   j __ t

i

ch __ n   l __ ps   s __ ck   s __ t

o

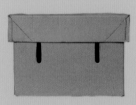

f __ x   b __ x   cl __ ck   l __ g

u

j __ g   h __ g   c __ p   n __ t

Middle letters

Write in the missing letters that make
the middle sounds of these words.

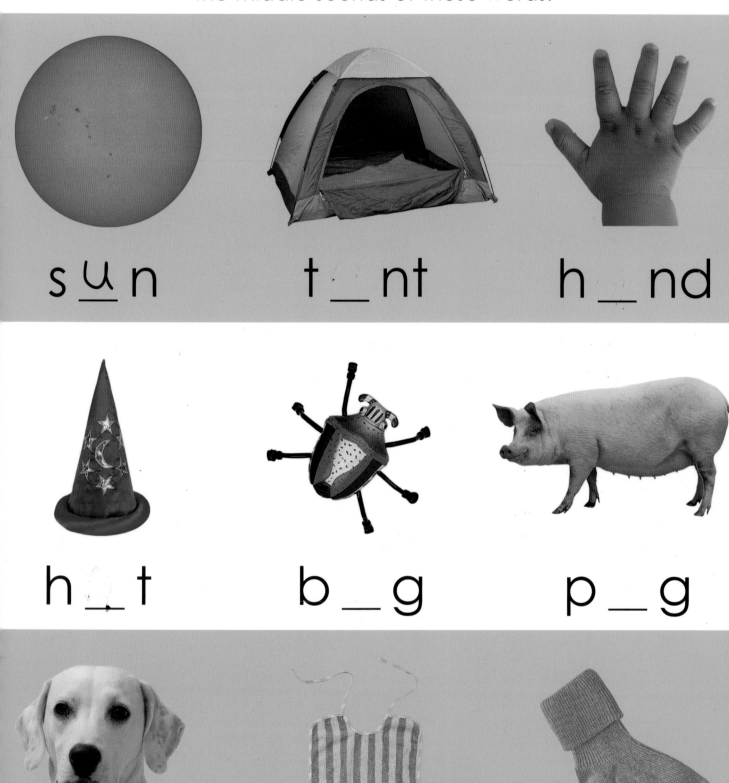

s u n

t _ nt

h _ nd

h _ t

b _ g

p _ g

d _ g

b _ b

s _ ck

Double letters

Use the double letters **ee** or **oo** to complete the words.

b e e

j _ _ _ p

m _ _ _ n

tr _ _ _

wh _ _ l

thr _ _ _

b _ _ k

sp _ _ _ n

sh _ _ p

Double letters

Use **pp**, **tt**, **dd**, **rr**, **ss**, **mm**, **dd**, or **bb** to complete the words.

 pu p p p y

 ra __ __ it

 ki __ __ __ en

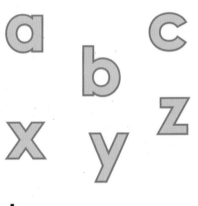 le __ __ __ ers

 bu __ __ __ les

 ca __ __ __ ot

 mo __ __ __ y

 da __ __ __ y

 ki __ __ __

Same sounds

The letters **ee** and **ea** make the same sound.
Choose the right one to complete each word.

p <u>e a</u> ch

str _ _ _ t

_ _ gle

s _ _ side

l _ _ ves

asl _ _ _ p

d _ _ r

t _ _ th

s _ _ l

Same sounds

The letters **ow** and **ou** make the same sound.
Choose the right one to complete each word.

fl <u>ow</u> er

＿ ＿ l

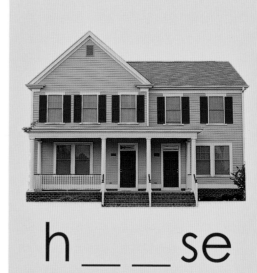

h ＿ ＿ ＿ se

sh ＿ ＿ t

t ＿ ＿ ＿ el

m ＿ ＿ ＿ se

t ＿ ＿ ＿ er

sp ＿ ＿ ＿ t

tr ＿ ＿ ＿ el

Rhyme time

Complete the words, and then cross out the object in each row that does not rhyme with the others.

h <u>a</u> <u>t</u>   c _ _   f _ _ _ _   b _ _ _

m _ _   p _ _   c _ _   b _ _ _

Draw a line between each pair of rhyming words.

map   fig   sun   fox

leg   cap   hen   run

pen   box   pig   peg

Math

Practice number

Trace the numbers, and then practice writing them on the lines.

1

2

3

4

5

6

7

8

9

10

11

12

13

14

15

16

17

18

19

20

1 to 5

Count the objects and write the totals in the boxes.

1 truck

flowers

piglets

dogs

cows

6 to 10

Count the objects and write the totals in the boxes.

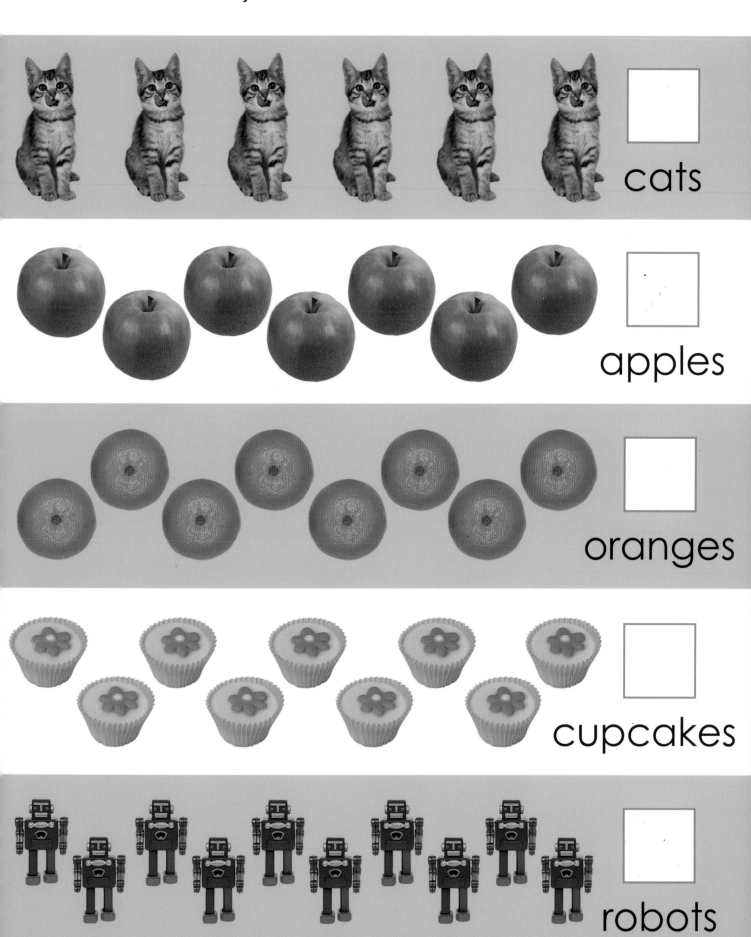

cats

apples

oranges

cupcakes

robots

Adding 1

Add **1** to the first group of objects to find the totals.
Write the answers in the boxes.

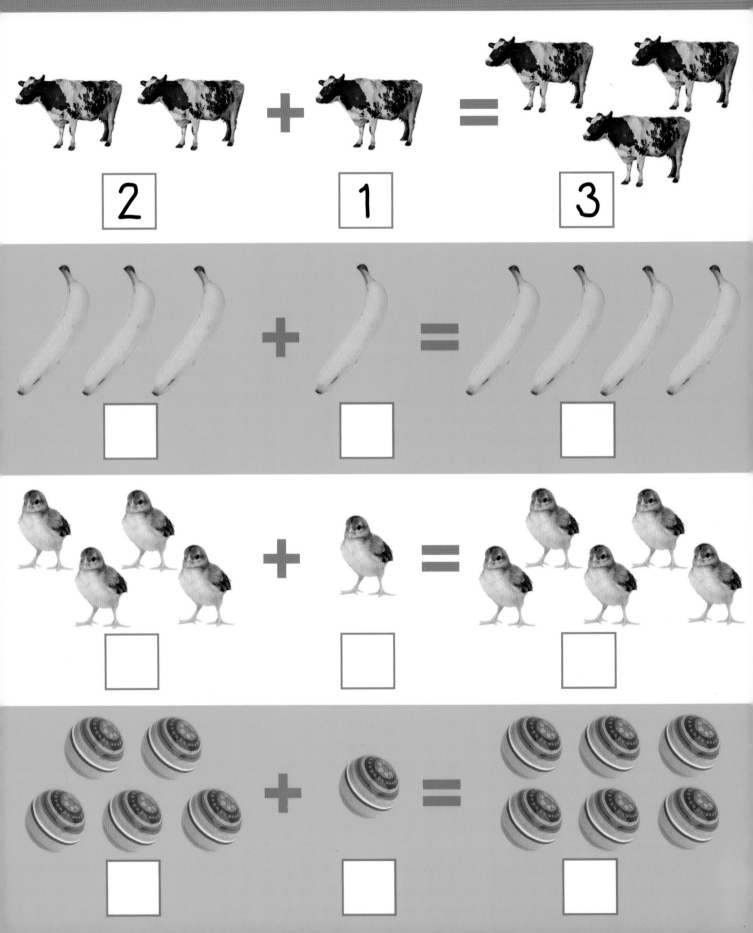

2 + 1 = 3

Subtracting 1

Subtract **1** from the first group of objects to find the totals.
Write the answers in the boxes.

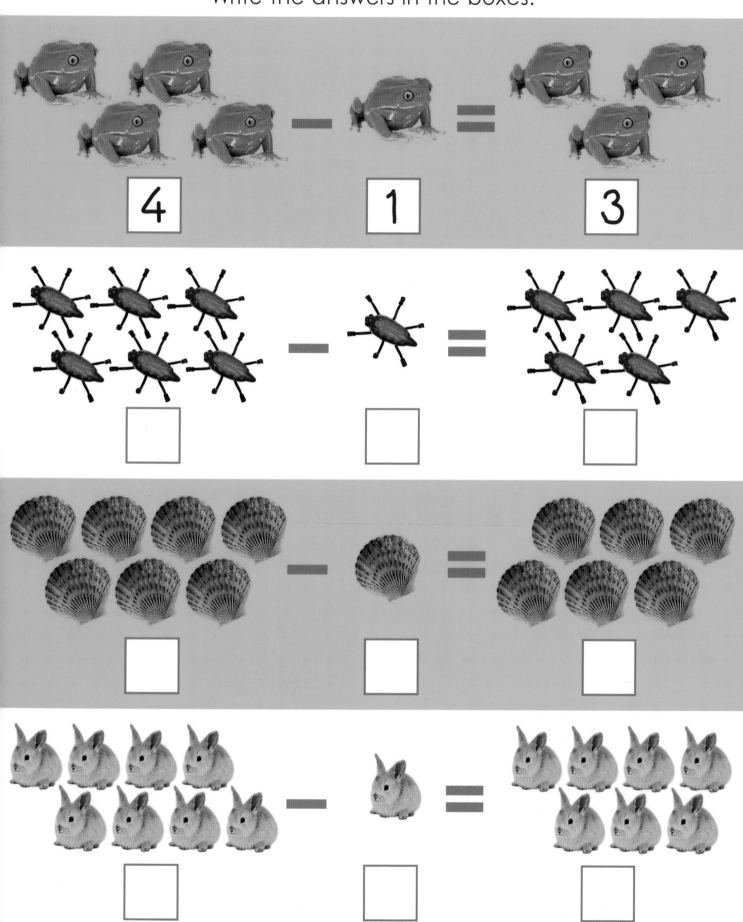

| 4 | | 1 | | 3 |

Adding groups

Write the amount of each group in the boxes,
and then add the groups together.

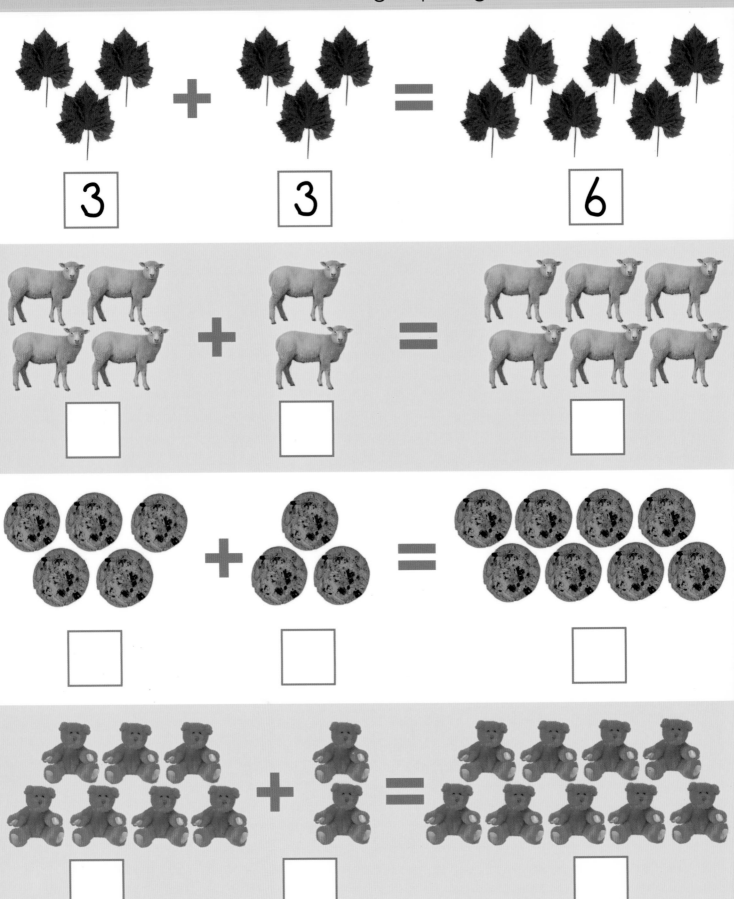

Subtracting groups

Write the amount of each group in the boxes.
Subtract the second group from the first.

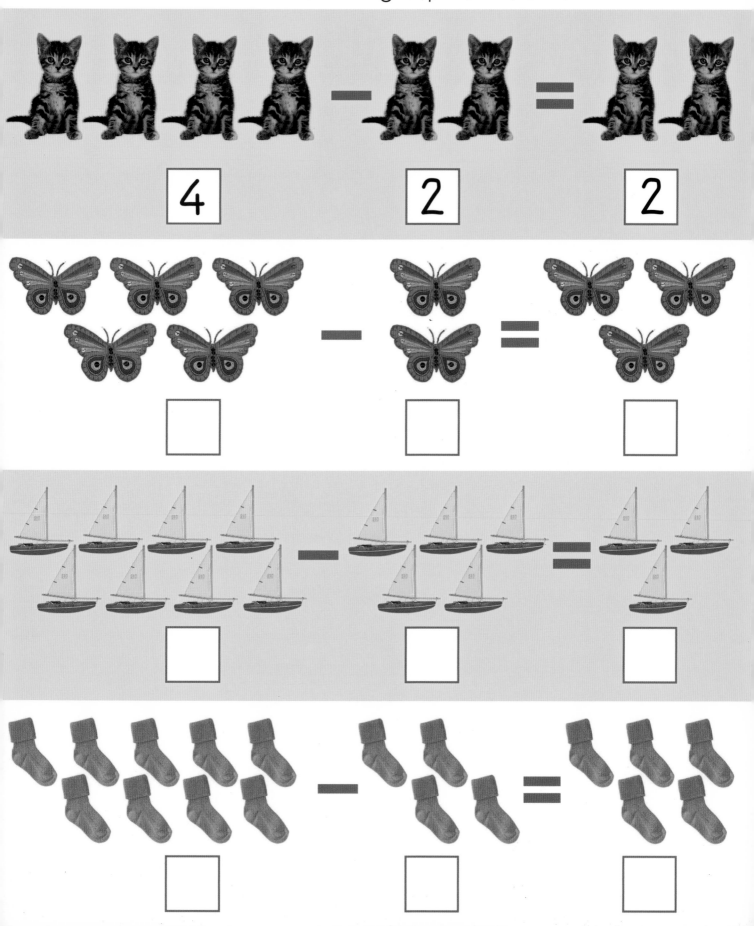

4   —   2   =   2

Subtracting to 5

Try these different ways of subtracting to make 5.

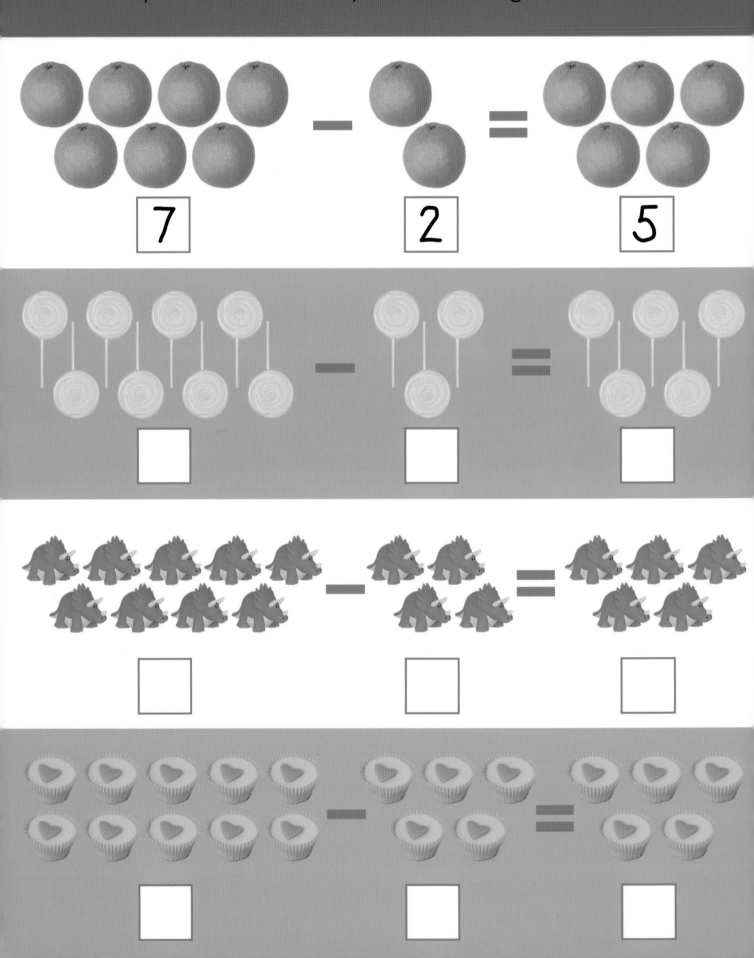

Adding to 10

Try these different ways of adding to make 10.

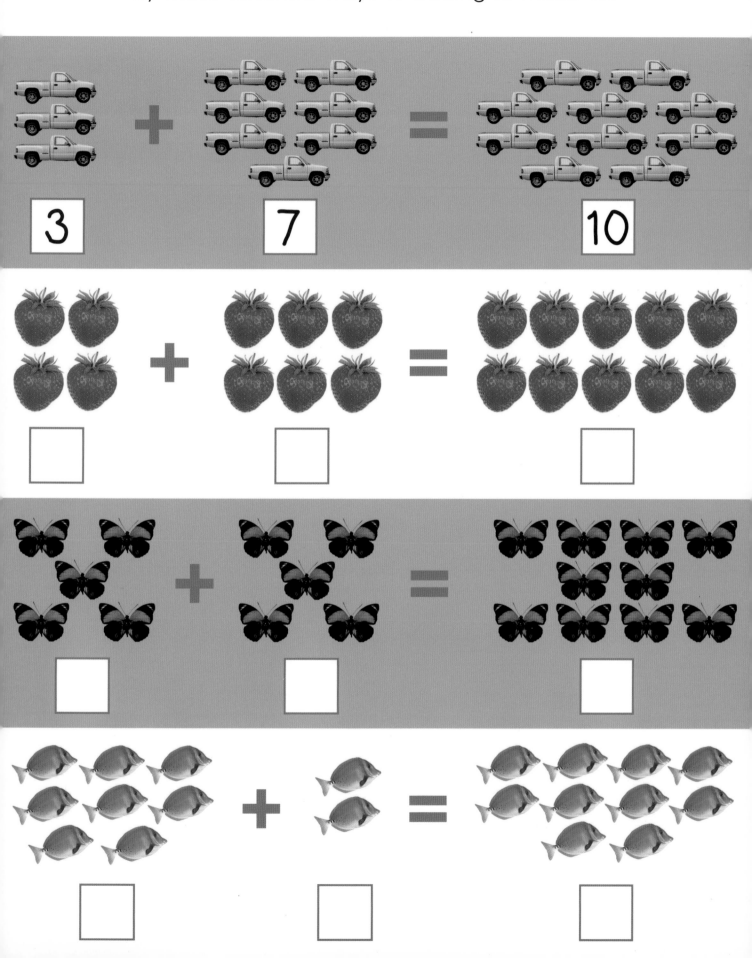

Doubling numbers

To double a number, add the same number to itself.

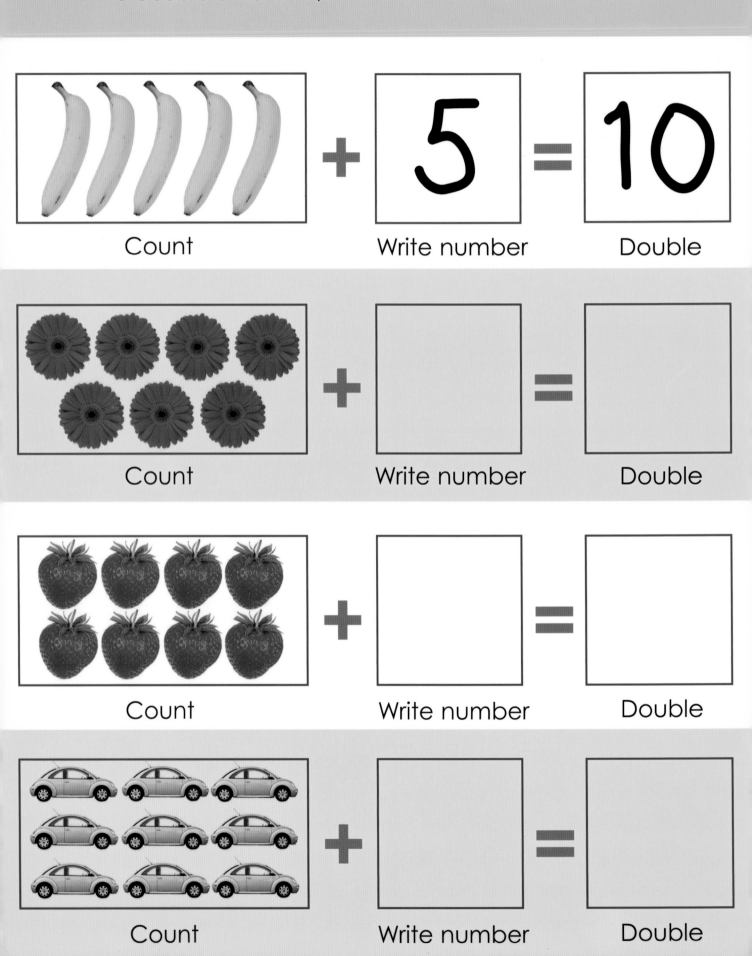

Count   +   Write number **5**   =   Double **10**

Count   +   Write number   =   Double

Count   +   Write number   =   Double

Count   +   Write number   =   Double

Halving numbers

When you halve a number, the amount you take away is the same number that's left over.

Cross out the objects to make

half of 4

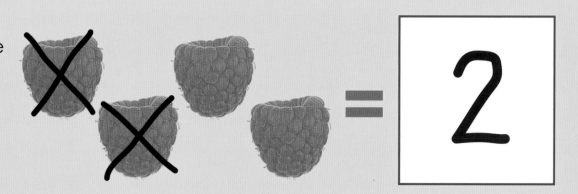 = 2

Cross out the objects to make

half of 6

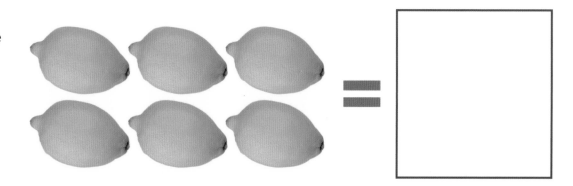 =

Cross out the objects to make

half of 8

 =

Cross out the objects to make

half of 10

Practice page

Parents: Use this page to help your children practice their
math and give them new exercises to try.

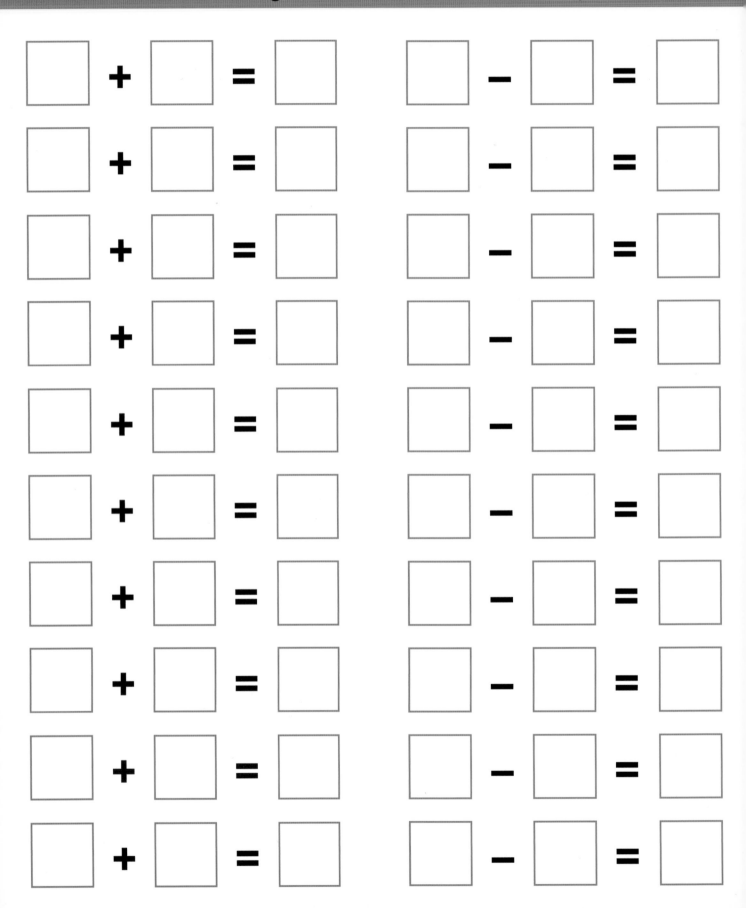

Puzzles

Missing letters

Fill in the missing first, middle, and last letters.

__ eaf

__ -shirt

__ ag

bl __ ck

s __ oe

h __ t

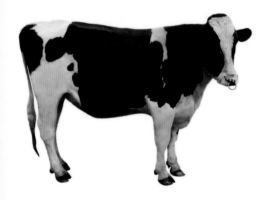

co __

lim __

ca __

Missing letters

Fill in the missing first, middle, and last letters.

_ _ hair

_ _ ar

_ _ amb

sh _ _ rts

c _ _ mb

b _ _ ok

duc _ _

bow _ _

lam _ _

What's different?

There are six differences between these two beetles.
Circle the differences on picture B when you find them.

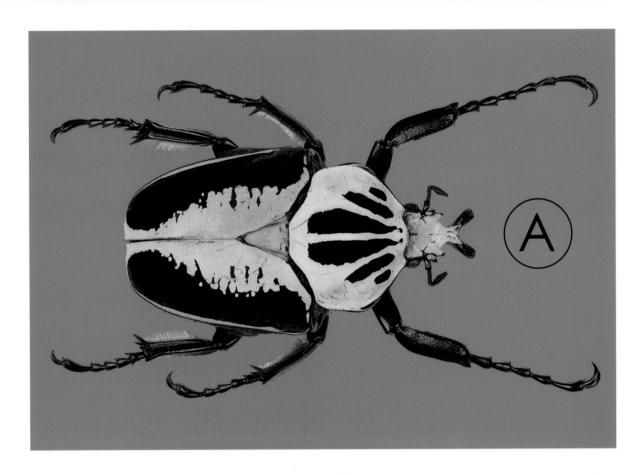

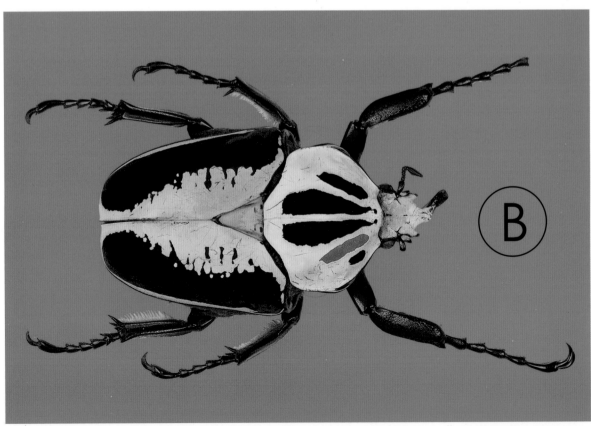

Flower maze

Can you find a way through the maze
to help the butterflies reach the flower?

start

finish

Bug crossword

Use the picture clues to help you write
the names of the bugs in the crossword.

3 down

¹b ²f

³b

3 across

1 down

⁴s

⁵a

⁶s

4 across

2 down

5 down

6 across

Sudoku squares

Fill the numbers 1, 2, 3, or 4 into the empty squares. Each number must appear once in each row, column, and box of four squares.

Look at this example:

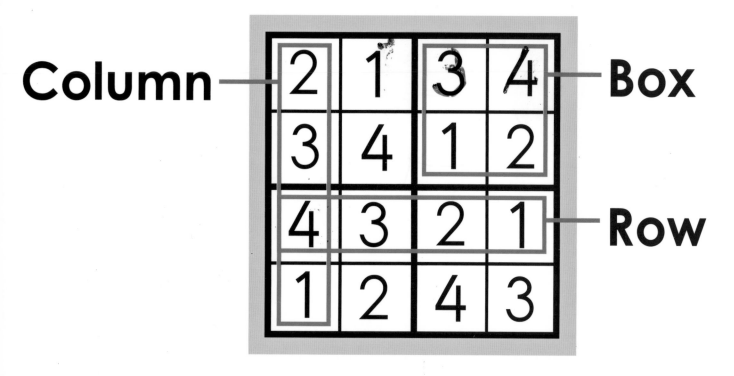

Column

Box

Row

Now try the sudoku puzzles below.

Word puzzle

Use the picture clues to help you make
words from these mixed-up letters.

I eat carrots. <u>r a b b i t</u> **btirab**

I have claws and a shell. _ _ _ _ _ **rcab**

I make a "meow" noise. _ _ _ _ **tca**

I am round and colorful. _ _ _ _ **lalb**

What noise do I make?

Trace over the noises, and then draw a line
to link each noise to the correct animal.

Sudoku squares

Fill the numbers 1, 2, 3, or 4 into the empty squares. Each number must appear once in each row, column, and box of four squares.

Look at this example:

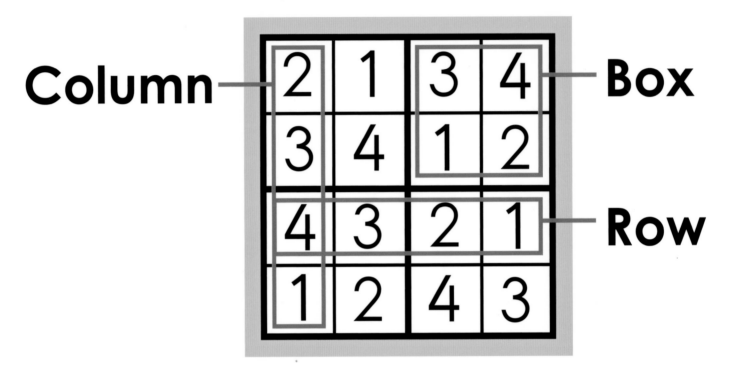

Now try the sudoku puzzles below.

Chicken trail

Which path will take the chicken to her chicks?

bunny

chicks

piglet

What's different?

There are six differences between these two diggers.
Circle the differences on picture B when you find them.

Space maze

Can you find a way through the maze
to guide the rocket back to Earth?

start

finish

Connect the dots

Connect the dots to finish the pictures.
Can you name the animals?

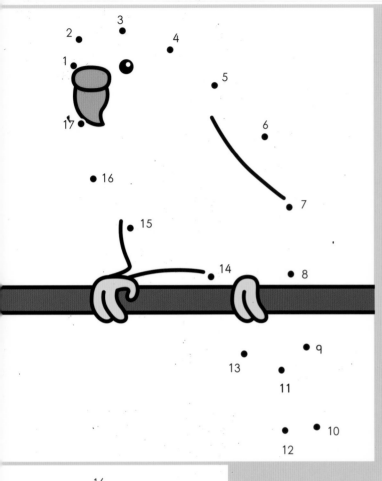

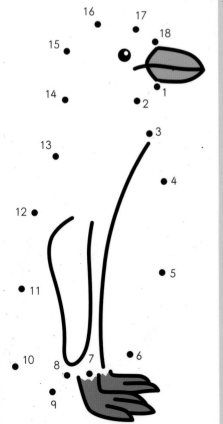

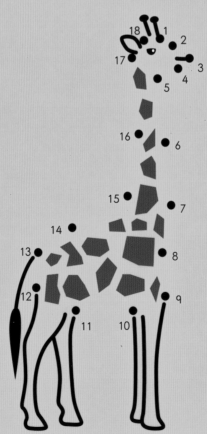

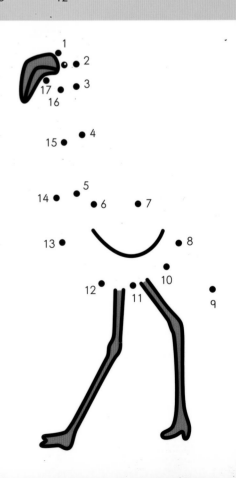

Fun with numbers

Follow the instructions below.

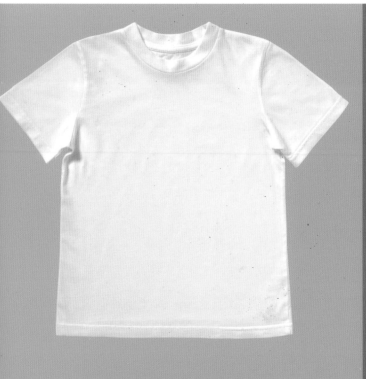

Draw three stripes
on the T-shirt.

Draw six spots on the ladybug.

Give the car two wheels.

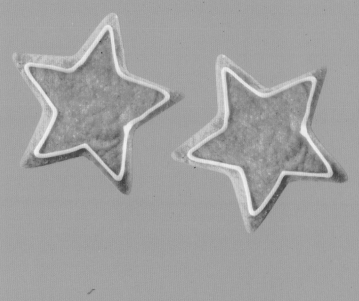

Draw one more star.

Word puzzle

Use the picture clues to help you make
words out of these mixed-up letters.

I am a red flower. r o s e **sero**

I travel in the sea. _ _ _ _ _ **btao**

I have green leaves. _ _ _ _ _ **tere**

I have a hard shell. _ _ _ _ _ _ **nsial**

Rainbow words

Trace over the names of the colors, and then draw a line from each color to where it appears in the rainbow.

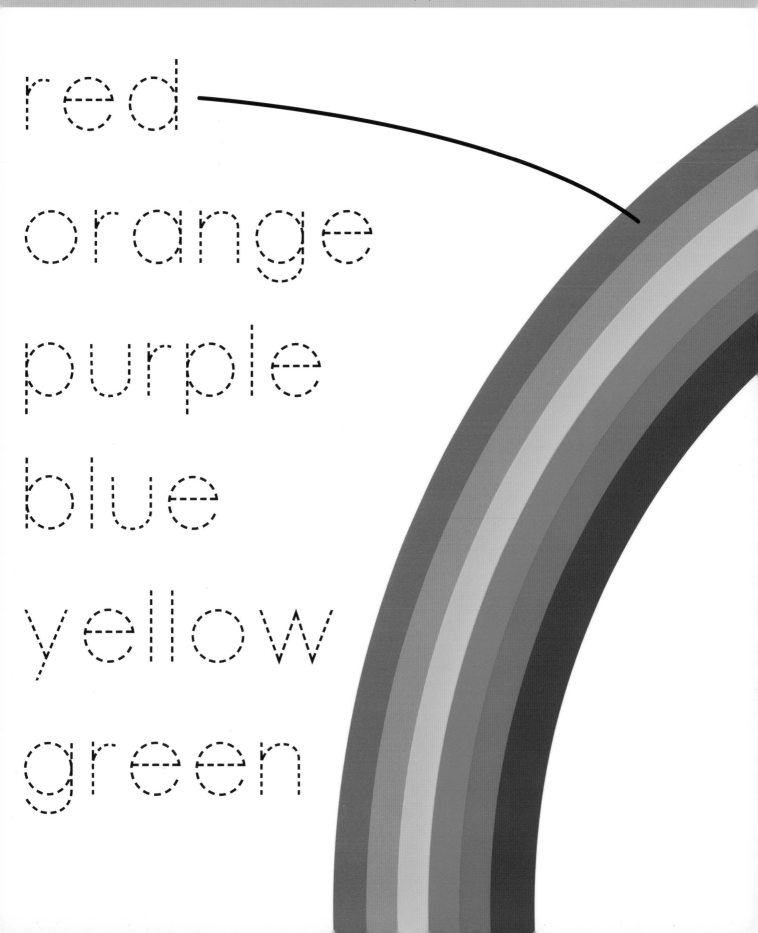

red

orange

purple

blue

yellow

green

Pond maze

Can you find a way through the maze to
lead the ducklings to their mommy?

start

finish

What's different?

There are four differences between these two giraffes.
Circle the differences on picture B when you find them.

Connect the dots

Connect the dots to draw the space shuttle.

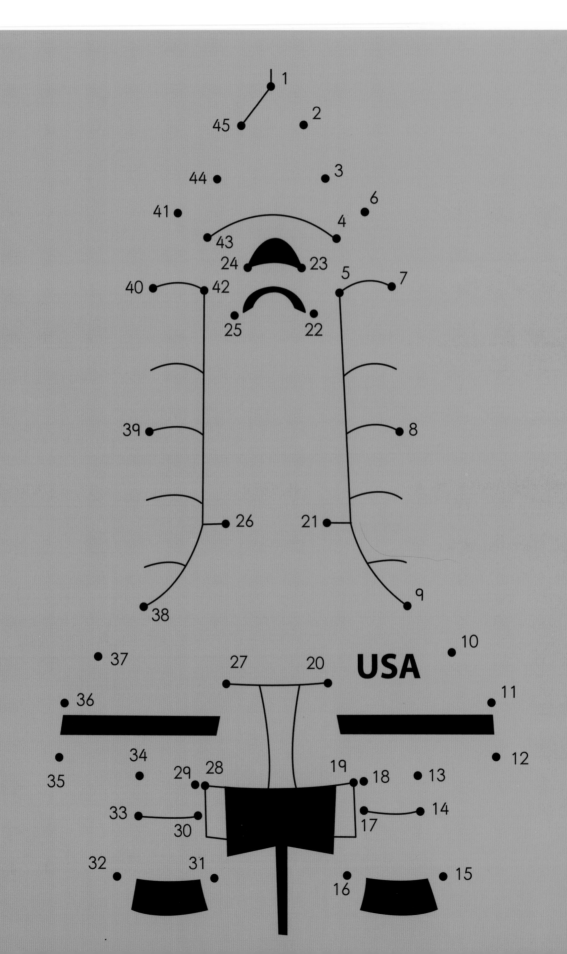

Sudoku squares

Fill the numbers 1, 2, 3, or 4 into the empty squares. Each number must appear once in each row, column, and box of four squares.

Look at this example:

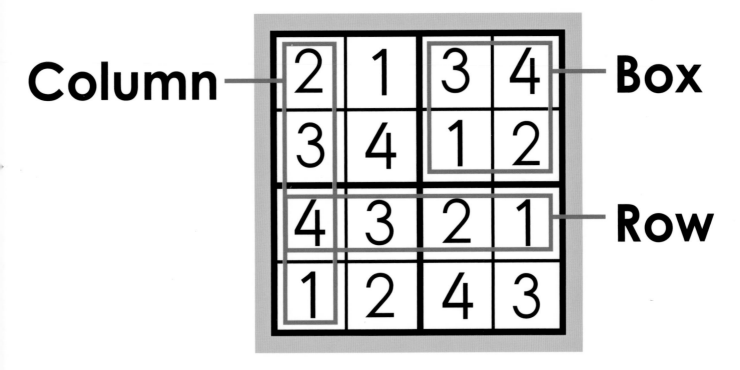

Now try the sudoku puzzles below.

What's different?

There are five differences between these two tractors.
Circle the differences on picture B when you find them.

Truck word search

Can you find the names of the trucks written below in the box?

d	u	m	p	t	r	u	c	k	e
a	y	u	a	a	m	k	t	a	a
r	p	i	c	k	u	p	r	t	r
e	h	n	t	f	n	r	z	r	w
s	w	e	i	o	i	b	l	a	r
p	h	a	p	s	t	i	r	c	y
t	i	p	p	e	r	g	l	t	b
d	b	d	x	r	m	r	o	o	w
e	u	g	t	h	u	i	n	r	i
s	s	z	s	l	i	g	c	f	g

tractor

big rig

dump truck

bus

tipper

pickup

Connect the dots

Connect the dots to draw the astronaut.

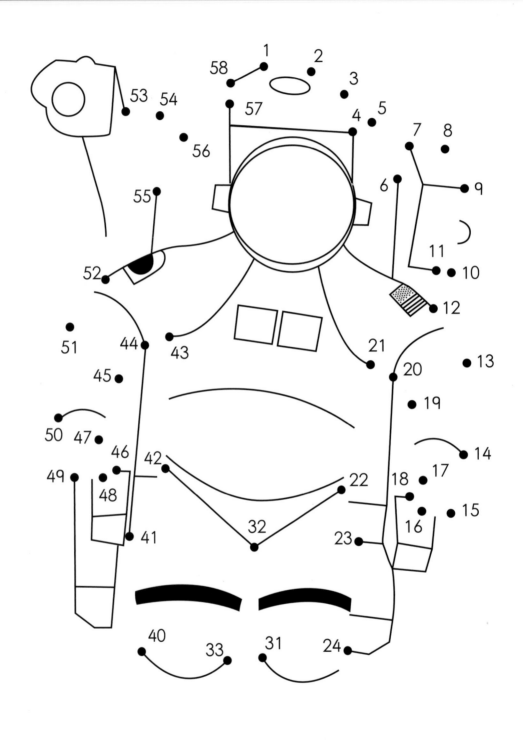

Beach crossword

Use the picture clues to help you write
the beach words in the crossword.

2 across

1 down

3 across

4 down

5 across

Sudoku squares

Fill the numbers 1, 2, 3, or 4 into the empty squares. Each number must appear once in each row, column, and box of four squares.

Look at this example:

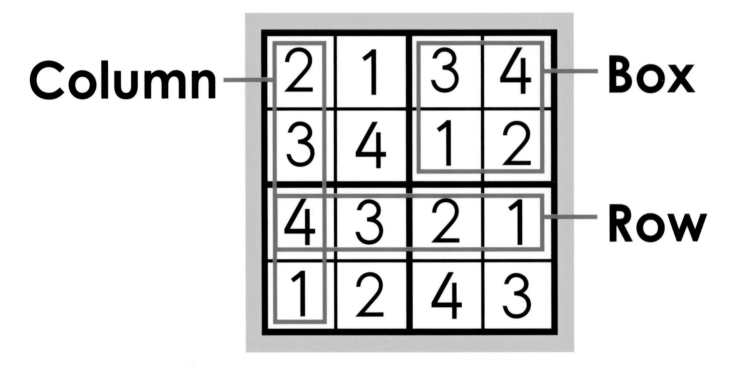

Column **Box**

Row

Now try the sudoku puzzles below.

Pets word search

Can you find the names of the animals written below in the box?

d	o	g	t	e	r	f	l	y	e
a	y	u	a	a	m	k	t	a	a
r	e	i	n	n	i	d	r	n	r
e	h	n	t	f	o	r	z	c	w
l	w	e	o	i	z	x	l	c	r
o	h	a	m	s	t	e	r	o	a
i	y	p	s	h	e	m	t	u	b
d	a	i	x	r	m	h	o	r	b
t	q	g	t	h	u	e	n	t	i
r	c	z	s	l	i	f	c	a	t

 guinea pig

 fish

 dog

 rabbit

 hamster

 cat

Zoo crossword

Use the picture clues to help you write the names
of the zoo animals in the crossword.

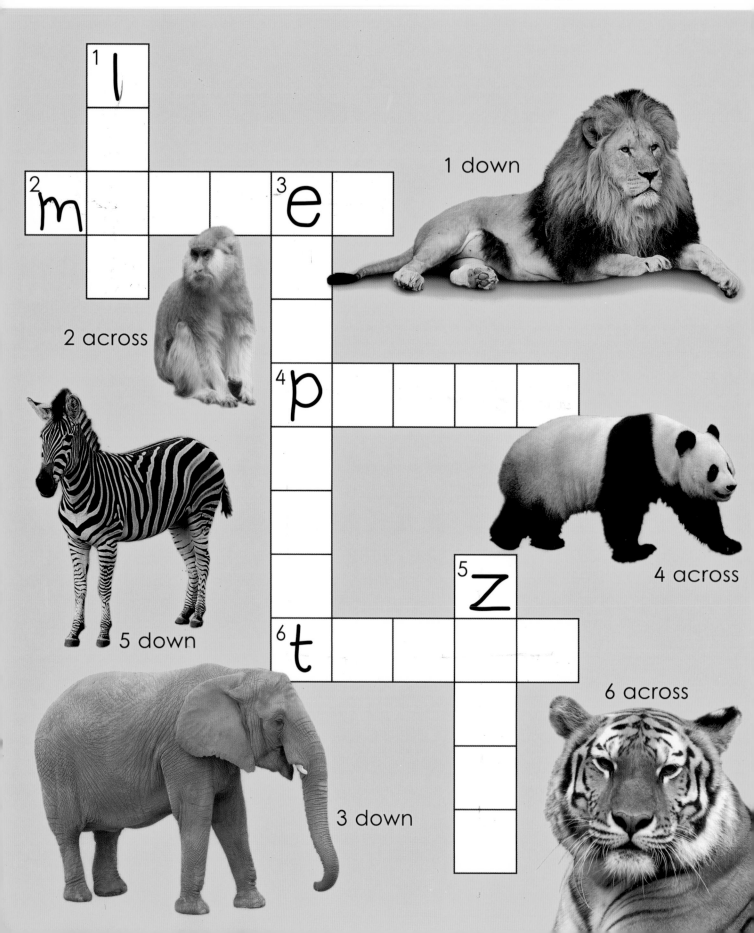

1 down

2 across

4 across

5 down

5 Z

6 across

3 down